SCIENTIFIC AMERICAN EDUCATIONAL PUBLISHING

LIGHT IT UP!

10 FUN PHYSICAL SCIENCE EXPERIMENTS WITH LIGHT

BRING SCIENCE HOME

Published in 2023 by Scientific American Educational Publishing in association with
The Rosen Publishing Group 29 East 21st Street, New York, NY 10010

Contains material from Scientific American, a division of Springer Nature America, Inc., reprinted by permission as well as original material from The Rosen Publishing Group.

First Edition

Editor: Natalie Humphrey
Designer: Rachel Rising

Activity on page 5 by Science Buddies/ Sabine De Brabandere (June 6, 2019); Activity on page 13 by Science Buddies/ Svenja Lohner (October 25, 2018); Activity on page 19 by Science Buddies/ Sabine De Brabandere (October 11, 2018); Activity on page 25 by Science Buddies/ Megan Arnett (April 26 2018); Svenja Lohner (January 18, 2018); Activity on page 31 by Science Buddies/ Svenja Lohner (March 30, 2017); Activity on page 35 by Science Buddies (November 24, 2016); Activity on page 39 by Science Buddies/ Sabine De Brabandere (October 27, 2016) ; Activity on page 45 by Science Buddies (May 5, 2016); Activity on page 50 by Science Buddies (February 18, 2016)

Photo Credits: pp. 3, 4, 5, 9, 16, 22, 28, 33, 35, 37, 38, 42, 43, 48, 54, 55, 59, cve iv/Shutterstock.com; pp. 4, 5, 13, 19, 25, 31, 35, 39, 45, 50, 55 Anna Frajtova/Shutterstock.com.0

All illustrations by Continuum Content Solutions

Cataloging-in-Publication Data
Names: Scientific American.
Title: Light it up!: 10 fun physical science experiements with light / Scientific American.
Description: New York : Scientific American Educational, 2023. | Series: Bring science home| Includes bibliographic information, glossary and index.
Identifiers: ISBN 9781684169757 (pbk) | ISBN 9781684169764 (library bound) | ISBN 9781684169771 (ebook)
Subjects: LCSH: Experiments-- Juvenile literature | Light-- Juvenile literature | Physics-- Juvenile literature | Science projects-- Juvenile literature
Classification: LCC QC360 S35 2023 | DDC 535 --dc23

Manufactured in the United States of America

CONTENTS

⚛ THESE ACTIVITIES INCLUDE SCIENCE FAIR PROJECT IDEAS.

INTRODUCTION

Light can play some fun and wild tricks on not only your eyes, but also the world around you! Have you ever seen a colored shadow before? Or wondered where a rainbow comes from? Fun-shaped mirrors make your reflection goofy, but how do they work? To answer that, we need physics!

Projects marked with  include a section called Science Fair Project ideas. These ideas can help you develop your own original science fair project. Science fair judges tend to reward creative thought and imagination, and it helps if you are really interested in your project. You will also need to follow the scientific method. See page 61 for more information about that.

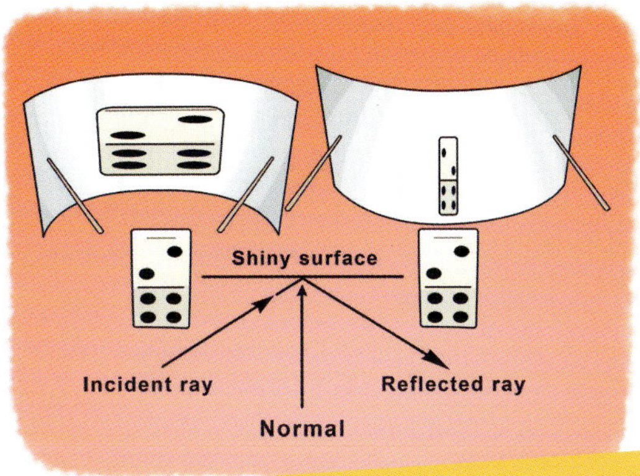

Distorted Images

CAN YOU ALWAYS TRUST WHAT YOU SEE? LEARN HOW PHYSICS CAN EXPLAIN WACKY FUN HOUSE MIRROR EFFECTS!

Have you ever visited a house of mirrors and seen a wacky-looking version of yourself? In this activity you can construct your own miniature house of mirrors. Try it out and see what funny reflections you can make!

PROJECT TIME

15-20 minutes

KEY CONCEPTS

Physics
Optics
Light
Reflection

BACKGROUND

We see an object when light reflected from the object shines into our eyes. From that input of light, the brain uses the eyes' signals to reconstruct a picture of the object.

The brain makes a few assumptions in this process of reconstructing a picture. One assumption is that the light rays traveled in a straight line from the object to the eye. Although a light ray usually travels in a straight line, in some cases it can change direction first—for example, when a light ray enters or leaves a transparent material, such as water, or bounces off a shiny material, such as a mirror. Your brain still runs the usual reconstruction process, treating the image as if it were created by rays that traveled in a straight line. As a result, your brain might reconstruct a picture that looks different than the original object; your brain might have been fooled!

Light reflecting off of a surface is kind of like a ball bouncing on a floor. If the floor is flat and you drop the ball straight down, the ball will hit the floor and reverse direction, bouncing straight up. This direction is called "the normal" to the surface. If you drop the ball at an angle to this normal, it will bounce back at the other side of the normal, but with the same angle to the normal. The same principle applies to light reflecting (or bouncing back) from a surface. In this case, the ray of light approaching the surface is known as "the incident ray." If the incident ray strikes the reflective surface at a particular angle, the reflected ray leaves the surface at the same angle—but is located at the other side of the normal. In other words, the incident and reflected ray make a perfectly symmetrical V shape, with the normal as the line of symmetry.

Mirrors reflect almost all of the light hitting their surface. In addition, they have a very smooth surface and are usually flat, causing light to reflect in an orderly way, reflecting a good but "mirror image" of objects. This results in a neat image on the retina and thus a clearly reconstructed picture. Shiny surfaces that are not perfectly smooth can lead to blurry or fuzzy pictures.

Mirrors make it possible to see a picture of yourself or of objects that are behind you. But do they always give an accurate representation of how you or the objects behind you look? Try the activity to see how mirrors can fool you!

MATERIALS

- Mirroring paper, available from a craft or paper supply store. New, unwrinkled aluminum foil can be used, but because the images are fuzzier, the observations will not be as clear.
- Old flip-flop that can be damaged. If unavailable, use an old insole or thick cardboard.
- Two skewers
- Small colorful objects, such as figurines, small toys, a battery, an eraser, etc. (If you are using aluminum foil, it is helpful to choose brightly colored objects.)
- Stainless steel spoon, as new as possible (optional)
- Glue (optional)
- Stainless steel cups, pots, ladles, etc. (optional)

PREPARATION

- To make a bendable mirror, cut a rectangle of your mirroring paper to cover the sole of the flip-flop (or other backing you will use).
- Lay the flip-flop on the table in landscape orientation (so that the long side is parallel to the side of the table), sole side up.
- Place the rectangle of mirroring paper on top with the mirroring side facing up.
- Carefully stick one skewer through the mirroring paper into the flip-flop an inch or so from the right edge, and stick the second skewer a few centimeters from the left edge of the flip-flop. The skewers should stick straight up from the flip-flop.
- If needed, use glue to keep the skewers in place.

PROCEDURE

- Turn your mirror on its side so the long side rests on the table, mirrored side facing you. Place a small object on the table in front of the mirror. If your object is skinny and tall, lay it on its side. *Can you see the reflection in the mirror?*

- Compare the reflection of the object in the mirror to the object. *Do they look identical? Are the size and color the same? Do they appear to stand at the same location?*

- Push the sides of the mirror back so the middle bulges out toward you. This type of curved mirror is called a convex mirror. Compare the reflection of the object in the convex mirror to the object. *Do they look identical? If not, how do they look different?*

- Let the mirror go back to being flat, and then push the middle backward and the sides forward so the middle of the mirror caves in. This type of curved mirror is called a concave mirror. Compare the reflection of the object in the concave mirror to the object. *Do they look identical? If not, how do they look different?*

- Repeat the previous three steps with a few other objects. *Do you observe similar things each time? When do objects elongate or become shorter? In what direction do they change?*

- The skewers stick straight out from the mirror. Scientists call this line the normal to the surface. *Do you see that for a flat mirror they are parallel to each other?*

- Look what the skewers do when you create a convex mirror. *Are they still parallel to each other? If not, do the tips of the skewers get closer to each other or spread out more?*

- Create a concave mirror and look again. *Are the skewers parallel to each other? If not, do the tips of the skewers get closer to each other or spread out more?*

- Incident and reflected light rays always make a perfectly symmetrical V shape with the normal as a line of symmetry. For a flat mirror the normals (represented by the skewers) are parallel. For a concave or convex mirror, the normals point inward and outward, respectively. This is similar to what is happening with the light rays: they come together when the mirror bends inward (concave) and move apart when the mirror bulges out (convex). *Can you use this knowledge to explain the distortions seen in the reflections in a concave and convex mirror?*

- Take the mirror in your hands, hold it in portrait orientation (so it is tall and narrow) in front of you. *Can you see your face? How do you think your face will look if you curve the mirror one way, and then the other way?*

- Bend the mirror to make it a convex mirror. *How does your face look in a convex mirror? Was your prediction correct?*

- Bend the mirror to make it a concave mirror. *How does your face look in a concave mirror? Was your prediction correct?*

EXTRA

Our mirrors curved along one direction. *What do you think the reflection would look like if it curved in all directions, like a spoon does?* Try mirroring yourself or a small object in the outside of a metal spoon. (The newer the spoon, the clearer the image will be.) *What do you observe? What do you think will happen when you mirror yourself or an object in the inside of the spoon?* Try it out. *Was your prediction correct?*

EXTRA

Take a small object and move it away from and then closer to the inside of the spoon. Now bring it very close—until it is almost touching. *Is the reflection still upside down when you have the object close? Why do you think this would happen?*

EXTRA

Take your homemade mirror and bend it into a concave shape. Bend it quite far and estimate the point where the skewers would touch if they were long enough. Maybe your skewers do touch! Place an object closer to the mirror than that point, and one farther away. Adjust your position and the position of the objects so you can see the reflection of the objects in the mirror. *Can you see what is strange about the reflection of the object farther away? Can this help you find out when the reflection in a concave mirror is reversed, and when it is not?*

EXTRA

Take small objects and see what their reflections look like in shiny stainless steel cups, pots, ladles, etc. *Can you understand what you see?*

OBSERVATIONS AND RESULTS

Did you see distorted reflections in the curved mirrors? Light rays that shine off a point on an object travel in all directions. Those reaching the mirror bounce back like a ball would bounce on a smooth surface. Some will travel into the eye. The location where these reflected light rays or their extensions meet is where the brain thinks the object is, so that is where the object appears to be when you see it in the mirror.

For the flat mirror, the skewers, which represent the normal to the surface, are parallel to each other. This creates reflected rays that meet at a point behind the mirror so the image appears at the other side of the mirror. For a flat mirror, the reflection is the same size and appears at the same distance from the mirror as the actual object.

For a convex mirror the skewers pointed outward. In this case light rays bounce the same way with respect to the normal but because the skewers point away from each other, the rays seem to spread out more compared to the ones reflecting on a flat mirror. These rays also meet at a point behind the mirror, but not as far behind it as the flat mirror. An object reflected in a convex mirror appears closer to the mirror and smaller than it really is.

For a concave mirror the skewers point toward each other, and the reflected light rays spread out less. The reflection of an object close to the mirror is bigger and looks farther away. If the skewers were long enough, they would have met at a point before the mirror. Move the object closer to the point where the skewers meet, and the reflected rays will spread out less. As a result the object will seem bigger and farther away. The reflection gets so big that your mirror probably only covers a fraction of it. Once you cross the point where the skewers meet, something strange happens: you see the object inverted! The right and left sides (if your mirror is in landscape orientation) or top and bottom (if you hold the mirror in portrait orientation) of the image are switched! This happens because the light rays meet before the mirror, so a light ray that starts at the right or the top will reflect back toward the left or the bottom. The inside of the spoon is curved in the horizontal and vertical direction, so right and left sides and top and bottom of the image are switched.

CLEANUP

Make sure to throw your bent foil and put away up any toys, spoons, and pans you took out.

Change the Size of a Shadow!

WHAT'S CASTING THAT SHADOW? LEARN HOW YOU CAN CHANGE THE APPEARANCE OF A SHADOW WITH SOME SIMPLE PHYSICS.

During Halloween, every corner seems have a spooky shadow! Luckily this is all they really are—just shadows that are part of decorations set up to give you a thrill while trick-or-treating. But where do these shadows come from, and how can some of them be so huge? Do this activity and find out how to generate the largest and scariest shadow of all!

PROJECT TIME

10-15 minutes

KEY CONCEPTS

Physics
Optics
Light
Shadow

BACKGROUND

You need some kind of light source to generate a shadow. This can be the sun, a lamp, or a flashlight. All light sources emit light waves that travel away from them. In optics, which is a special field of physics, this emitted light is modeled as a straight line called a light ray, which indicates the direction in which the light travels.

To cast a shadow you need an object that can block light rays. Not every object is able to do that. Some materials will let the light pass through, whereas others will only block some of it. Objects able to block all the light are called opaque and will form a shadow. You also need a large surface such as a wall or screen on which you can make the shadow visible.

How can you vary the size of a shadow? The closer an object is to the light source, the larger the shadow it casts. This is because an object closer to the source will block a larger area of the light, increasing its shadow size. Try it out for yourself in this activity!

MATERIALS

- Two measuring tapes
- Transparent tape
- Opaque objects that block light, such as a cup, toy car or ball
- Flashlight
- Table
- Light-colored wall
- Dimmed work space
- Paper
- Pen

PREPARATION

- Place a table right next to a light-colored wall.
- Tape the first measuring tape onto the table with the zero mark right at the wall.
- Select an opaque object that is able to fully block light rays from a light source. It shouldn't be too big or small.

- Put the flashlight on the table so it aligns with the measuring tape facing the wall. It should be located 20 inches (50 cm) away from the wall.
- Dim the lights in the room so it is dark enough to see clear shadows on the wall.

PROCEDURE

- Switch on the flashlight and point it to the wall. *What do you see on the wall once you switch on the light? How does the appearance of the wall change when you switch the light on?*
- Switch the flashlight off but do not move it. Take the object and place it next to the flashlight, 10 inches (25 cm) away. Then move it toward the wall until it is located 8 inches (20 cm) away from the wall. *What do you think you will see once you switch on the light?*
- Switch on the light and look at the wall. *Does the object placed on the table form a shadow? Can you explain why or why not?*
- Move the object directly between the wall and the flashlight so it sits on top of the measuring tape. Place it at the 8 inches (20 cm) mark of the measuring tape. *How will the shadow change once you move the object?*
- Switch on the light. *What do you see on the wall this time? What shape does the shadow have?* If there is a shadow, take the second measuring tape and measure the shadow's height from the table surface to its top and write its size on a piece of paper. *How big is the shadow?*
- Once you have measured the shadow's height, move the object closer to the wall along the measuring tape until it reaches the 4 inches (10 cm) mark. Then measure the height of the shadow again and record its size. *How does the size of the shadow change when you move it farther away from the light source? Do you notice any other differences besides the size?*

- Move the object closer to the flashlight and place it at the 16 inches (40 cm) mark on the measuring tape. Again, measure and record the height of the shadow. *Does the shadow get smaller or bigger when you place the object closer to the light source?*

- Look at your results on the piece of paper. If you like, you can make a graph that shows the distance from the light source on the x axis and the size of the shadow on the y axis. *How is the size of the shadow dependent on the distance of the object from the light source? Can you explain your results?*

EXTRA

Play around with different objects. Choose different materials or different sizes. Or make your own shapes! *Do they all form a shadow? Why or why not?*

EXTRA

Introduce a second light source by placing two flashlights in front of the wall. *How do the shadows of objects that you put in between both flashlights and the wall look? How do they differ from shadows using just one light source?*

EXTRA

Try to point your flashlight onto the object from different angles. *How does the angle change the appearance of the shadow?*

OBSERVATIONS AND RESULTS

Were you able to change the size of the object's shadow? Before you could change the size of the shadow you needed to generate it first. You probably didn't see a shadow when you placed the object next to the flashlight and not directly into its path of light. This is because light travels in a straight line and, because the object was not located in the direct light path, it could not block the light from its source. Once you placed the object directly in the path, however, you should have seen a shadow on the wall that had the same shape as the object. This time the opaque object was able to block the light from the light source, creating the dark shadow on the wall.

You should have observed the shadow's size decrease when you moved the object farther from the light source and increase when you moved it closer. You block a much larger portion of the light from the source when your object is closer, which increases the size of the shadow. Now you know how to make spooky Halloween shadows grow and shrink!

CLEANUP

Remove the tape from your measuring tapes and put them away. Make sure any flashlights you used are turned off and put away.

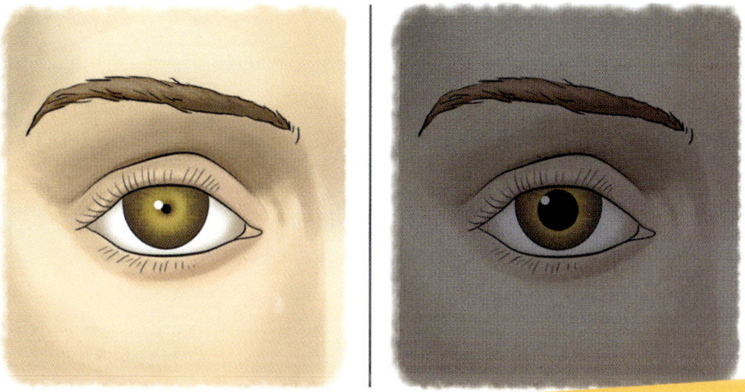

Seeing in the Dark

WHAT CAN YOU SEE? LEARN HOW OUR EYESIGHT CHANGES IN THE DARK

Have you ever considered taking a nighttime nature walk? Would you wait until there is a full moon so you could benefit from sunlight reflected from the moon—or would you rather take a flashlight? Do you think trees would look black, green, or gray in the dark? Try this activity to examine your night vision and prepare for your next nighttime adventure!

PROJECT TIME

10–15 minutes

KEY CONCEPTS

Biology
Vision
Pupil
Light
Color

BACKGROUND

Sight begins when light enters the eye. This light triggers light-sensitive cells in the retina at the back of the eye. As a result, signals zoom along the optic nerve to the brain. The brain then makes sense of the signals, giving us the experience of seeing.

The pupil is the opening in the middle of the front of the eye that allows light to enter. Humans have round pupils. They appear black because light almost never escapes through them. The colored part around the pupil called the iris adjusts the size of the pupil. Its main function is to regulate the amount of light that enters the eye. In dim light the pupils dilate (open wider) so more light can enter. Switch to bright light and the pupils automatically contract. This is the result of a nerve signal generated in the back of the eye triggering the muscles in the iris. Because some nerve connections cross over to the other eye, both pupils contract in unison.

MATERIALS

- Flashlight that shines white light
- Flashlight that shines red light (You can also hold a translucent red object such as a translucent red food container lid in front of the white flashlight to make it shine red light.)
- Room with a bright light (such as an overhead light) that can also get dark (nearly pitch-black works best)
- Markers, pencils, and pens of different colors and a bag to carry them in
- A volunteer or a mirror

PREPARATION

- Before we start you need to know what the pupil of an eye is. Look your volunteer in the eye or look at your eyes in a mirror. The dark circle in the middle of the eye is the pupil. In this activity, you will estimate the size of the pupils.

- Put a few markers, pencils, and pens in a bag, and bring it and your volunteer to a dark room.

PROCEDURE

- Allow your eyes to adjust to the dark for a few minutes. *How is your vision in the dark (also referred to as night vision)? Can you see anything and, if so, can you recognize items? Can you describe them accurately?*
- Let's test: Pick an object from the bag. *Can you and your volunteer see well enough to say what the object is? Can both of you identify the object's color?*
- Repeat previous step with another object from the bag. *Are the results identical?*
- In a moment you will switch on the light and immediately look at your volunteer's pupils or your pupils in the mirror. *Do you think anything special will happen to the pupil?*
- Turn on the room's bright light and quickly observe the pupils. *How large were they when you just turned on the light? How large are they when the light is on for a while? Why do you think this change happens?*
- *How do you rate your vision when there is plenty of light?* To test this, take an object from the bag and hold it in the light. *Can you recognize it? Can you see details such as its color?*
- Turn the light off and let your eyes adjust to the dark.
- Turn on your flashlight on the white light setting. Hold it close enough so that you can clearly see your volunteer's eyes, but take care not to shine the light into them or look directly into the beam of light. *What happens to the pupil size when you turn on the light?*

- *How well can you see what this white beam of light illuminates? How well can you see what is not directly in the light beam?*
- To test, take an object from the bag and hold it in the light. *Can you recognize it? Can you see details such as its color? What happens when you hold it away from the beam of light?*
- Repeat the previous four steps, but instead of a white beam of light choose a red light beam. *Do you expect your vision will be different when you have a red beam of light instead of a white one? If so, how and why do you expect it to be different?*

EXTRA

Find an adult to accompany you on a night outing to an area where there is very little light pollution. *How easily can you do a night walk with your flashlight off, with it on the red-light setting, and with it on the white-light setting? How is the experience different? Does the number of stars you can observe depend on the color light you use?*

EXTRA

By wearing an eye cover over one eye while exposing the other eye to bright light, you can investigate how bright light in one eye changes the pupil size of the other eye. *Do both pupils work in unison when they contract or expand, or does it happen independently?*

OBSERVATIONS AND RESULTS

Did the pupils expand when exposed to a low-light environment and contract when there was plenty of light? Were you able to recognize objects in dim light but unable to recognize their colors? That is what our eyes are designed for.

Pupil size changes to optimize vision in a large range of light conditions. When there is bright light a smaller opening in the eye—or a smaller pupil—protects the back of the eye from getting damaged. In dim light, the pupils dilate to allow as much light in as possible. That is why you see the pupils change size when light conditions change. Red light, however, does not trigger pupil contraction as much as other colors of light, making a red flashlight ideal for enjoying the night landscape.

Light-sensitive cells in the retina at the back of our eye allow us to see. The human eye has two types: cones and rods. Rods are extremely efficient; a tiny amount of light can trigger them. They are responsible for our night vision. They detect lines, contrast and movement—but they cannot distinguish color. The cones are responsible for color vision but they need plenty of light to activate. That is why in dim light conditions you could recognize an object but failed to detect its color.

CLEANUP

Put away any markers and flashlights, and say thank you to anyone that helped you with the project!

Make Your Own Rainbow

HOW MANY COLORS CAN YOU FIND OVER THE RAINBOW?

PROJECT TIME

20-25 minutes

KEY CONCEPTS

Physics
Wavelength
Refraction
Reflection

Did you know that in the U.S. we generally count seven colors in a rainbow whereas elsewhere in the world people only count five? We all see the same rainbows but it can be tricky to count the colors because they all blend together so seamlessly. So the next time you see a rainbow in the sky, try to count how many distinct colors you see!

If you don't want to wait that long, you can count the colors in the mini rainbow you create yourself in this activity! With it, we can explore the physics of light that creates these beautiful "rainy arches."

BACKGROUND

In addition to being beautiful, rainbows serve as a wonderful example of visible light's dispersion and its wavelength spectrum. Visible light travels in the form of a wave, much like sound and ocean waves do. Similar to how we hear different sounds depending on their wavelengths, we see different light wavelengths as a spectrum of colors from red to blue, which is how we can pick a yellow jelly bean out of bowl full of different-colored candies. The colors of the visible light spectrum are often referred to as ROYGBIV, which stands for: red, orange, yellow, green, blue, indigo, and violet. This is the order of the wavelengths of visible light starting with red (the longest) and ending with violet (the shortest). It is also the order that colors appear in a rainbow!

Rainbows appear when sunlight shines through water droplets suspended in the atmosphere. Each water droplet behaves like a small prism, refracting the light and reflecting it back to our eyes. When sunlight enters a water droplet, it is first refracted (bent as it enters the water droplet) then reflected by the internal surface of the water droplet so that it turns around at (very approximately) a 90-degree angle, and then it is once again refracted when it leaves the water droplet and reenters the air. That's a lot of bouncing around!

Light refraction is a term for the way light bends as it enters different mediums. You can observe light refraction firsthand by filling a clear glass with water and then looking through the glass. Everything on the other side of the glass appears slightly misshapen. This is due to the bending of light as it enters the far side of the glass, travels through the water, and then exits the other side of the glass before it reaches your eyes.

Different wavelengths of light bend differently. Shorter ones (such as blue and violet) bend slightly more than longer wavelengths (such as red and orange). When white light (which contains all colors of light) enters a water droplet and then leaves it again, each different wavelength of light refracts at a slightly different angle. As a result, the white light is broken up into its component parts and we can see all of the colors in the form of a beautiful rainbow!

MATERIALS

- Shallow glass baking pan
- Water
- White sheet of paper
- Red sheet of paper
- Blue sheet of paper
- Sunlight
- Outdoor table, chair, or helper to hold the pan for you

PREPARATION

- Fill your pan about halfway full of water.
- Take your pan outside and place it on the table so one end sticks out over the table edge. Be careful not to let the pan tip over! You can use either another pan or your helper to anchor the pan in place.

PROCEDURE

- Place your white paper on the ground, where the sun is shining through your pan. *What do you notice about the appearance of the water on the paper? Do you see any colors?*
- Slowly change the angle of the sheet until a small rainbow forms. Test the angle of the paper until you get the largest rainbow possible. *What paper position works best for a rainbow? What position makes it most difficult to see a rainbow? Which colors are the clearest in the rainbow? Which are the most difficult to see?*
- Notice the order of the colors that appears on the paper. *What color is at the bottom of the rainbow? What color is at the top?*
- While holding your white paper so you can view the rainbow, place your blue paper gently on top of the white one. *What do you notice about the rainbow on the blue sheet? Does it get easier to see or more difficult?*
- Switch back and forth between the white and blue sheets and notice how the rainbow changes. *Which colors are easiest to see with the blue paper? Which are more difficult to see? Which colors are easiest to see with the white paper? Which are more difficult to see?* Test each sheet and note whether it is easier to see colors on the top of the rainbow or the bottom.

- Remove the blue paper, but keep the white one in place so you can still see your rainbow. Gently place the red paper on top of the white one. *What do you notice about the rainbow on the red sheet? Does it get easier to see or more difficult?*
- Switch back and forth between the white and red sheets, and notice how the rainbow changes. *Which colors are easiest to see with the red paper? Which colors are more difficult to see? Which colors are easiest to see with the white paper? Which are more difficult?* Test each paper and note whether it is easier to see colors on the top or bottom of the rainbow.

EXTRA

Use colored pencils, crayons or markers to color in the rainbow that you see on your white, blue, and red papers. Use a clipboard to hold the paper steady and fill in the colors of the rainbow you see on each sheet. Compare the colors you draw!

OBSERVATIONS AND RESULTS

In this activity you created your own mini rainbow. Even though yours was much smaller than the ones you see in the sky, both rainbows are created by the same principles: light reflection and refraction.

We know refraction refers to how light bends when it passes through different mediums or materials such as glass, water, or plastic. When the sunlight shines through the water of your glass pan, the light bends. Because white light (such as sunlight) is made up of all of the visible colors, this means they all bend. Because those different colors of light have different wavelengths, they bend at slightly different angles. The water effectively breaks up the white light into its different colored components. This light reaches your paper and you see all the different colors reflected.

You should have noticed the light you observed in your rainbow changed depending on the color of your construction paper. Note that the changes you observed depend on the shade of blue and red papers you used. If you found slightly different results than these, that's okay! Try testing other colors of paper to see what other results you find.

With the white sheet of paper, you should have been able to see all of the colors clearly. This is because white paper reflects white light—and as we know, white light is made up of the whole spectrum of visible light. Therefore, all of the colors could be observed in your rainbow. When you used the blue paper you might have observed some of the colors appeared a little crisper. If you had an easier time seeing your rainbow with the blue paper, this might have been because you didn't see as much of the water reflected on the blue sheet as you did on the white one. The water's reflection on the white paper can make it more difficult to see your rainbow clearly. Instead of reflecting all light, like white paper does, blue paper absorbs some of the colors and reflects others. Generally, the blue dye on the paper absorbs red light, allowing some green and all blue light to be reflected. Because many visible colors in the rainbow are made up of some green and blue light (including some shades of yellow and pink, which have green and blue light in them), the rainbow colors you see on your blue paper might have looked similar to those you observed on the white paper.

When you used the red paper, however, you might have observed a significantly different rainbow. The red dye on the red sheet absorbs blue and green light and only reflects red light. Because green and blue make up a large part of the visible rainbow, removing these colors leaves us with a pretty bland looking version. You probably couldn't see many colors except for some orange and red at the very bottom of your rainbow.

CLEANUP

Pour the water from your pan down the drain or into the garden, and put away your materials.

Turning Soot into Silver—with Science!

NOW YOU SEE IT—NOW IT'S CHANGED! EXAMINE HOW LIGHT CHANGES WHEN YOU CHANGE THE SURFACE OF AN OBJECT.

You might have heard the saying "not everything is as it seems." Something far away might look great, but when you take a closer look it might not turn out to be as you thought it would be! In this activity you will turn a spoon blackened with soot into shiny silver. Even though it is only an illusion, you will not know it when you see it. Try it out for yourself!

PROJECT TIME

15-20 minutes

KEY CONCEPTS

Physics
Light
Reflection
Vision

BACKGROUND

How do we see what we see? Vision is based on light—without light we would not be able to see anything. Light travels in waves that eventually reach our eyes, where signals are sent to our brains, which translates these signals into information such as the color, location or appearance of an object we are looking at. When light waves strike an object, they can interact with it in several ways: They can be reflected back like those from a mirror; they can be absorbed, which means they are captured by the object; they can be transmitted and pass through it; or they can be scattered and deflected in different directions. Additionally, light that passes through a transparent object such as air, water or glass can also be refracted, which means the light wave bends when it passes from one transparent substance into another. Without this bending of light due to refraction we would not be able to use lenses or magnifying glasses.

How light interacts with an object depends mostly on the properties of its material. Objects that absorb most of the light appear dark or opaque. If an object has a very smooth surface, the light can be reflected and bounces off of the material's surface. One example is a mirror's smooth surface, which reflects light at an angle equal to that of the incoming light wave. This is the reason why we see ourselves in the mirror—the image reflected by the flat surface is reproduced. Rough surfaces reflect light as well, but they reflect it in more than one direction. The incoming light wave is scattered from the surface in all directions because the surface is uneven. In this activity you will see for yourself how a material's surface can determine how light interacts with it. The result will surprise you as the exact same object can appear in very different lights—literally!

MATERIALS

- Adult helper
- Candle
- Matches or a lighter
- Two metal spoons (that you have permission to use)
- Glass
- Water
- Paper towels
- Black permanent marker
- Nail polish remover

PREPARATION

- Fill the glass halfway with water and place it next to your candle.
- Color the back of one spoon with the black permanent marker.

PROCEDURE

- Take the metal spoon that you have colored with black permanent marker. *Can you clearly see the black color on the back of the spoon?*
- Put the metal spoon that has been colored into the glass of water and look at it from all angles. *Is the spoon still black underwater? Does the appearance change from different viewing angles?*
- Next, take the other metal spoon and observe its appearance. *How does it look? Is it very shiny?*
- Ask an adult helper to light the candle, and observe the burning candle. *What does the flame look like? Do you see any soot coming from the flame?*
- Next, hold the back of the metal spoon in the top part of the yellow flame. *Does the appearance of the spoon change? If yes, how does it change? Can you explain what happened?*
- Once your spoon is covered in soot, let it cool for a minute. Observe the spoon's surface. *Does its black surface look rough or smooth?*
- After the spoon has cooled, slowly submerge it into the glass of water. Then look at it from different angles. *How does the back of the spoon look? Can you see the black sooty surface under the water? Does its appearance change with different viewing angles?*
- Finally, slowly take the spoon out of the water and look at it again. *Does the spoon look different? Is the soot still black? Does it look wet?*

EXTRA

Test if the activity works with objects other than a spoon. Make sure, however, that the objects you choose are heat-resistant and you have permission to test them. Try to cover a heat-resistant plate or an eggshell with soot. *Can you create the same illusion with different objects?*

OBSERVATIONS AND RESULTS

A metal spoon looks very shiny because its surface is very smooth, which is why it acts like a mirror and reflects light very well. If you paint it with black paint, it looks black. This doesn't change when you put the painted spoon in water. It still looks black from all angles.

When you put the metal spoon into the flame, however, you should have observed that after awhile the spoon turned black. This is because the candle produces soot from its wax that is made up of carbon and hydrogen. The yellow region of the flame contains tiny carbon particles that are deposited on the metal surface. Under a microscope you would see the soot on the spoon looks very bumpy and rough, almost like a mountain landscape. The surface looks black because, due to its roughness, any light that reflects from one particle will hit another one and get absorbed.

Once you put the black spoon into the water, however, you should have observed the previously black surface suddenly looked shiny and silver. Why is that? The answer is that due to the surface roughness of the soot, tiny air bubbles get stuck on its surface when you submerge the spoon in water. That means, on top of the soot there is a very thin layer of air bubbles. This air layer creates a very smooth surface on top of the rough soot surface. When light hits the boundary between the water and air layer, it is no longer absorbed but reflected in the same way as a mirror—the surface looks shiny. This phenomenon is also called "total internal reflection," which can only happen at the border between two different materials the light passes through—in this case water and air. When you take the spoon out of the water the spoon looks black again because the light once more is absorbed by the rough, sooty surface. With the painted spoon, there is no water-air boundary underwater because no air bubbles get stuck to the paint. That is why you do not see this phenomenon with the painted spoon.

CLEANUP

Remove the soot from the spoon using a paper towel. Use nail polish remover to remove the permanent marker from the other spoon. Make sure to extinguish the candle flame and clean your work space.

Sunset Colors in a Glass

WHY IS THE SKY BLUE DURING THE DAY—BUT CAN BE A BEAUTIFUL RAINBOW OF COLORS AT SUNSET? GRAB A FLASHLIGHT AND GET READY TO MAKE YOUR OWN SUNSET TO FIND OUT!

Have you ever watched a sunset and wondered why the sky suddenly changes from blue to orange and red? Even during the day the sky can have multiple colors ranging from bright blue to gray or white. Where do these colors come from? In this activity you will find out—and simulate your own sunset in a glass! Ready to watch the sun go down?

PROJECT TIME

20-25 minutes

KEY CONCEPTS

Light
Physics
Color
Wavelength

BACKGROUND

The majority of light that reaches Earth from space comes from the sun, which is our planet's principle light source. Light that comes from the sun is called white light, although it is actually a combination of all colors. You can see these colors in a rainbow when white light is separated into its individual colors by raindrops. Each color is characterized by a certain wavelength as light travels through space in waves. Some wavelengths are shorter and have more energy, such as blue light; some are longer with less energy, such as red light.

If these waves hit an object, they can interact with the object in several ways: they can be reflected back from the object like those from a mirror; they can be absorbed, which means they are captured by the object; or they can be scattered and deflected in different directions.

What does this all have to do with the color of the sky? The answer is that before the sunlight reaches Earth, it first has to travel through our atmosphere, which is a layer of gas made up of tiny molecules of mostly nitrogen and oxygen that surrounds our planet. When sunlight travels through the atmosphere, the white light interacts with these gas molecules and is scattered in all directions. Not all wavelengths of light are scattered the same way, though. Shorter wavelengths, such as blue light, are scattered much more than the longer ones. This scattered blue light is what we see and what makes the sky look blue.

When the sun sets, it is much lower in the sky, which means that the sunlight has to pass through more air in the atmosphere to reach your eyes. This causes greater scattering of the blue light. The remaining wavelengths that you see are now longer ones that get less scattered, such as orange and red. Small particles in the air enhance the scattering effect, which is why on hazy days or when there is air pollution, the sunsets appear even redder. Want to see for yourself? Then try this activity, and turn white light into a sunset!

MATERIALS

- Tall glass or jar (at least 16 ounces [473 ml])
- Water
- Milk
- Teaspoon
- Bright flashlight that emits white light
- A workplace that can tolerate water spills

PREPARATION

- Fill your glass or jar to the top with tap water.
- Assemble your materials at your workspace.

PROCEDURE

- Shine your flashlight through the glass of water from the side. *When you look at the glass from the front, what does the water look like? What color is it? Can you see the light traveling through the water? Is the light beam narrow or wide?*
- Add about 1 teaspoon (5 ml) of milk to the water and stir until mixed. *How does the water look now? Is it still clear or does it look cloudy?*
- Take the flashlight and point it at the solution from the side. *Does the solution change color? If yes, why do you think the color change happened? What color do you see? Can you still see the light traveling through the solution?*
- Instead of shining the flashlight through the side of the glass, now place it on top of the glass and shine it through the solution from the top. *What changes when you shine the light from the top through the solution? Does the color of the solution look the same throughout the glass or is it different at the top compared with the bottom? Can you explain your observations?*

EXTRA

What happens if you add more milk to the water? Repeat the activity with different amounts of milk. *Do you still see the same colors as before? What changes when you add more milk to the water?*

SCIENCE FAIR PROJECT

Can you replace the milk with other substances and still get the same results? Try different solutions from your kitchen and find out! *What do all these substances have in common?*

OBSERVATIONS AND RESULTS

Did you see a sunset in your glass or jar? With only water in your container, you should have seen a clear solution. Even when you shine your light through, its color and appearance does not change much. You might have seen the light beam traveling through the water, which should have been relatively narrow, as the light does not interact much with the water molecules. If you add milk to the water, the solution changes. Milk is an emulsion, which means it consists of many tiny insoluble fat particles that are dispersed in the solution. This is why, after adding the milk to the water, the solution becomes cloudy.

When you point your flashlight at the milk-water mixture from the side, the light waves interact with the tiny particles in the solution and get scattered the same way sunlight does by gas molecules in the atmosphere. As blue light gets scattered most, your solution should have appeared slightly blue. Shining light from the top through the solution increases the distance the light waves have to travel through the water-milk mixture. That means the blue light can be scattered even more throughout the solution. This is why at the bottom of the glass there is almost no blue light left anymore—it looks yellow or orange instead. With the blue light scattered away, the solution should turn from whitish-blue at the top to a yellow-orange color at the bottom—just like a sunset!

CLEANUP

Pour the milk-water solution down the sink, clean up any spills, and wash your hands.

Be Seen in the Dark

BRIGHT AT NIGHT? YOU KNOW WHAT COLORS ARE EASY TO SEE DURING THE DAY—BUT WHAT ABOUT AT NIGHT? TEST OUT DIFFERENT HUES AND MATERIALS AND SEE WHAT WOULD MAKE YOU MOST VISIBLE!

PROJECT TIME

10-20 minutes

KEY CONCEPTS

Physics
Light
Reflection
Visibility

Being outside in the evening can be relaxing as well as exciting and fun, but it can also be dangerous—especially if you are around roads. At dawn, dusk, and during the night, it is difficult for drivers to see pedestrians. But do you think the types of clothes worn could make a difference in how visible pedestrians are to drivers? You probably know that camouflage makes you blend into the background. So, would wearing regular, noncamouflage materials be enough to make you more visible at night? Or would you choose to wear bright colors, fluorescent colors—or clothes with retro-reflective strips? This science activity will help you find out!

BACKGROUND

Humans "see" when light that reflects off of objects reaches our eyes. Some colors send more light back so we see them better. For example, brightly colored objects reflect more light than dark-colored objects do. Fluorescent objects send out visible light when high-energy light shines onto them. Retro-reflective material—often referred to as reflective material, used on road signs and some safety gear, for example—bounces back almost all of the light that shines onto it.

At night, there is little light available to bounce off of objects. Typical nighttime light sources (headlights or street lights) rarely contain high-energy light, the type that makes fluorescent objects so bright in daylight.

In this science activity you will put three different "colors" (bright, fluorescent, and retro-reflective) to the test. Which one do you think will increase visibility most in poor light conditions?

MATERIALS

- At least two grown-up assistants—one to work with you as an observer ("driver") and one to test out the different colors in the dark and play the role of a pedestrian.
- Black or dark clothing to cover most of the body of your adult tester
- Brightly colored garment or item for your adult tester
- Fluorescent garment or item for your adult tester
- Reflector or item equipped with retro-reflective tape for your adult tester
- Two or more flashlights, including one that is very bright (The more powerful your flashlight, the better! It is meant to mimic a car headlight.)
- An open space with little or no lighting after dark where it will be safe to test the clothing at night

PREPARATION

- Whenever you are out after dark, observe what you can see, and what is hidden until it is near you. Use these observations to make a hypothesis of which "color" will most increase the visibility of a pedestrian. *Will one "color" be way more visible from a distance? If so, why do you think this will be the case?*
- Before you go out after dark to perform the test ask your test assistant(s) to dress in black or a dark color. Take the three items or garments that the test assistant(s) will use and at least two flashlights with you to the test place.

PROCEDURE

- Have your observer ("driver") assistant(s) hold the brightest flashlight; stay alongside them to help rate the visibility of the test assistant.
- Have your test "pedestrian" assistant(s) take a flashlight and the three different "colors" of clothing and safely walk out to about 100 feet (30 m) straight ahead of the observer's flashlight—or until they are no longer very visible in their dark clothing. Once they arrive at a good distance for testing, have them flash a short on/off flashlight signal to alert the observer that it is time to rate the visibility.
- Now work with the observer to rate this "color" on a scale of 0 (not visible) to 10 (highly visible), imagining that you are in a car, and the flashlight is the headlight. Then signal back (again, a short off/on flashlight light signal) when done.
- The assistant can then take out (and/or put on) the brightly colored item and signal it is time to rate the visibility of that "color."
- Rate the visibility with the observer. *Were you surprised by this result?* Now use your flashlight to signal back for the test assistant to try a different color—this time the fluorescent one.

- Repeat the process again and then, finally, do the test with the retro-reflective item.
- *Is the difference in visibility of the different colors small, medium, or large? Can you find a reason why a color increases visibility at night?*
- *Was your expectation correct? Are you surprised by the results? Does this change what you might wear as a pedestrian at night or in low-light conditions?*

EXTRA

Have your assistants switch roles—or enlist additional observers. Compare the ratings of the different observers. *Do all agree that specific "colors" are more visible than others? Do they agree on which "colors" are most visible?*

SCIENE FAIR PROJECT

In this test you rated the visibility of pedestrians about 100 feet (30 m) away. *Do you expect the results to be the same at shorter or farther distances?* Perform a new test to find out!

EXTRA

Think about what else a pedestrian could do to increase his or her visibility at night. *Can you test these solutions in a similar way and compare these results with the ones you obtained in this activity? Did it increase visibility more, way more or less?*

EXTRA

Do you think pedestrians can accurately estimate how visible they are at night? To find out, ask people if they think a driver in a car can see them if they are dressed in the specific colors you tested. Compare their estimates with the test results you obtained.

SCIENE FAIR PROJECT

This test was performed at night in darkness. *How do you think results would change under low-light conditions, such as dawn or dusk? How would you design such a test?*

OBSERVATIONS AND RESULTS

Did you notice how much the retro-reflective materials aid visibility in the test circumstances?

Although more light bounces off bright colors than it does off dark colors, the difference is not enough to make a pedestrian visible at night from a car with headlights on. Putting on a fluorescent-colored item might help a little, as fluorescent colors send out visible light when high-energy light shines on them. Streetlights and car headlights, however, usually do not produce much high-energy light; the small amount they do shine slightly increases the visibility, which might have made the pedestrian faintly visible in your test. This visibility was probably tiny compared with that of a pedestrian equipped with retro-reflectors. Reflectors are very efficient at reflecting the light back and into your eyes, and can significantly improve visibility at night.

As you decrease the distance between the car and the pedestrian, the visibility of each of the colors increases. Still, at any distance, the retro-reflective material wins the visibility contest.

Most pedestrians overestimate their visibility on the road after dark sets in. They often correctly indicate retro-reflective clothing increases their visibility but underestimate its effectiveness.

CLEANUP

Turn off your flashlights and put away any clothes you took out. Make sure to say thank you to your assistants!

Serve Illuminated Water

CAN YOU BEND LIGHT WITH WATER? GRAB A FLASHLIGHT, TURN OUT THE LIGHT, AND FIND OUT!

PROJECT TIME

10-15 minutes

KEY CONCEPTS

Physics
Light
Reflection
Angles

Light is fascinating! It can look like a wave or a particle; it can be red, blue, or any color of the rainbow; you can even mix all the colors together to get white! It travels in straight lines and still appears to bend around objects. It can travel through air, but it does not need it. Unlike sound, light can travel from distant stars through a vacuum and reach us millions of years later or it can be sent through fiber-optic cables and circle the world in less than a second! Does that sound impressive? How about pouring light from a bottle into a glass or sink? Does this sound too far-fetched to you? Try this activity and make it happen!

BACKGROUND

Have you ever noticed how you need to point a flashlight toward an object to illuminate it? That shows light travels in straight lines. But what if we introduce a mirror or shine a light beam into water? Light bouncing off a shiny surface (in other words, reflected by the surface) or light bent when entering a medium (meaning refracted by the surface) introduces kinks into these straight lines. (Several activities listed in the "Extras" can help you understand these phenomena better.)

In this activity, you will look at what happens when light inside a body of water reaches the water's surface. Light falling nearly perpendicular on a water-air surface pierces through it; that is why we call water "translucent." But did you know that water also reflects part of the light? It almost acts like a mirror for light hitting it at small angles with the water's surface. When light initially hits the water-beam boundary at a small angle, it keeps hitting the boundary at small angles and is reflected over and over again. It can almost not escape to a less-dense medium, like air. This is called total internal reflection and explains how light gets trapped when it shines through water.

MATERIALS

- Flashlight
- Empty, colorless, transparent soda bottle (the one-liter size works well)
- Aluminum foil
- Water
- Dark room with a sink or tub

PREPARATION

- Place the flashlight at the base of the transparent empty soda bottle so that, when turned on, the light shines straight into the bottle, toward its neck.

- Wrap the bottle and flashlight in aluminum foil. Make sure you can still reach the flashlight's on/off button. Wrap the bottle to the rim, but leave the bottle opening unwrapped so you can still fill it with liquid.
- Find a room that can be darkened and also has a sink or tub into which you can easily pour water.
- Fill the prepared bottle with water

PROCEDURE

- Turn on the flashlight. In a moment you will turn off the room light. *What do you expect to see? Will the bottle glow? Will only the opening near the top glow? Do you expect the beam of light to illuminate the room, make a circle on the ceiling or not do much?*
- Turn off the room light and observe. *Was your prediction correct?*
- In a moment you will pour out the contents of the bottle into the sink or tub. *Do you expect to see anything special?*
- Tilt the bottle so water flows in a fluid arch into the sink or tub. (Turn on the room light briefly if you need to check where you are pouring the water.) Observe where the light goes. *Does the light travel in a straight line to illuminate the back of the sink, does it follow the water-beam to illuminate the bottom of the sink or does nothing much get illuminated? Is the water-beam glowing or hardly visible in the dark?*
- As the water runs out, observe where the light beam hits the sink or tub now. *Is it at a different spot? Why?*

EXTRA

If you have a laser pointer available, repeat the activity with it. (Be careful, though: Never look into the light produced by a laser or let the light bounce back from a reflective material into your eyes.) Before you repeat the activity with your laser pointer, explore the differences between the light produced by a laser and the light produced by your flashlight. *How are they different? How are they similar? How could these differences influence what you observed in this activity? Did the activity confirm or refute your predictions?*

EXTRA

Optical fibers are flexible strands of glass. They are used as cables to transport pulses of laser light (carrying information) over long distances. The light does not smoothly bend with the fiber, rather it frequently hits its wall. Each time the light hits the wall, it gets reflected back into the fiber. As long as you do not bend the fiber sharply, the laser light stays trapped in the cable all the way to its end. *Can you detect similarities between the activity and optical-fiber cables? Could you find ways to transmit information in your water-beam, and if so, how?*

OBSERVATIONS AND RESULTS

Did you notice how, at first, the light illuminated the spot on the ceiling or the wall where the bottle was pointing? Were you surprised to see how the light followed the beam of water when you poured the water?

Initially, when you are holding the water bottle up, the light emitted by the flashlight hitting the water surface is nearly perpendicular. In this case, light can easily move through the water surface and travel straight on to illuminate a spot on the ceiling or wall. Conditions change when you tilt the bottle and pour water out. Now, light hits the water surface at a small angle. In this case, the water surface reflects the light back into the water like a mirror would do. The reflected light travels on and encounters the water boundary again, at a different spot, but again at a small angle, and again it is reflected back. Time after time the light gets reflected at the edge of the water-beam. It is trapped inside the water-beam and follows the path of the water, only to be released when the water hits the sink or tub. There, light is reflected in all directions. You observe a brightly illuminated spot.

Light travels through optical cables in a similar way, continuously bouncing off the edges of the cable as it makes it way to the end of the cable, where it can release its information.

CLEANUP

Turn off the water. Throw away any tinfoil and recycle the bottles you used during the experiment.

Now You See It...Testing Out Light Refraction

MAKE A STRAW VANISH BEFORE YOUR EYES—WITH THE AMAZING DUO OF REFRACTING AND REFLECTING LIGHT. IT'S NOT MAGIC, IT'S SCIENCE!

PROJECT TIME

10–15 minutes

KEY CONCEPTS

Refraction
Reflection
Index of refraction

If you pour water into a clear glass, what color is it? It's clear, right? But what happens if you try to look through it to see the world on the other side of the glass? It looks a little distorted, maybe a little fuzzier and uneven. If water is clear, why can't we see through it clearly? The answer has to do with how light moves through water, glass and other transparent materials. Similar to when you try to run in a swimming pool, when light tries to move through water or glass it gets slowed down. When light is slowed down, it either bounces off the material or is bent as it passes through. We can see these changes in light, which indicates to us that something is there. In this activity you will play with light to make normal objects appear and disappear!

BACKGROUND

When light that is traveling through the air hits water, some of the light is reflected off the water. The rest of the light passes through the water but it bends (or refracts) as it enters the water. The same thing happens when light hits glass or any other transparent material. Some light is reflected off the object whereas the rest passes through and is refracted.

All materials have what is known as an index of refraction, which is linked to how fast light can travel through the material. As light passes through air and into another clear material (such as glass), it changes speed, and light is both reflected and refracted by the glass. This results in us seeing the glass because it reflects and refracts light differently than the air around it does. The change in the light allows us to differentiate one object from another. If a transparent object is surrounded by another material with the same index of refraction, however, the light will not change speed as it enters the object. As a result, you will not be able to see the object.

In this activity you will observe how the index of refraction of different materials helps us to see (or not see!) the objects as light passes through them!

MATERIALS

- Two clear glass jars, tall bowls, or drinking glasses that hold at least 8 ounces (237 ml) (Tip: Pyrex glass works well for this activity.)
- Vegetable oil, approximately 4 ounces (118 ml) or enough to fill one of the glasses halfway (Tip: Avoid using "light" vegetable oil for this activity.)
- Glass eyedropper (A plastic eyedropper or clear plastic drinking straw also will work. If you use a drinking straw instead of a dropper, each time you immerse the straw keep your finger over the top to avoid getting liquid in the straw. The instructions will tell you when to release your finger.)
- Other transparent glass objects, such as marbles, beads, a magnifying glass, or glass stirrers (optional)

PREPARATION

- Fill half of one jar with the vegetable oil.
- Fill half of the other jar with water.
- Make sure your eyedropper is clean before starting the activity.
- Set up a flat work surface that can be cleaned if any water or oil spills on it.

PROCEDURE

- Take your eyedropper (or straw) and, without squeezing it, immerse it in the jar of water. (For this step, avoid sucking up any water with the eyedropper or straw.) *What do you notice about the eyedropper? Can you still see it? How clearly?*
- Keeping the eyedropper in the water, squeeze the top to suck up water. If you're using a straw, release your finger from the top to allow the immersed straw to fill with water. *Did anything change about the eyedropper once it was filled with water? Does the eyedropper become easier or more difficult to see once it is filled with water?*
- Remove the eyedropper from the water and squeeze out all excess liquid.
- Immerse the eyedropper in the oil, without squeezing it. Make sure to avoid sucking up any oil for this first step. *What do you notice about the eyedropper? Are you still able to see it? Was it easier to see the eyedropper when it was in the water?*

- Squeeze the eyedropper to allow it to fill with oil. (If using a straw, remove your finger from the top to allow the immersed straw to fill with oil.) *What happened? Can you still see the eyedropper? Is it easier or more difficult to see it now than it was when it was empty?*

- Remove the eyedropper from the oil in the jar and squeeze out the excess oil.

- Slowly and gently pour the oil from the jar into the jar with the water. If you do this very carefully, the oil will sit right on top of the water! (It's ok if they mix though, they will separate once you stop pouring.)

- Allow the oil and water to settle and separate (about one to two minutes). *What do you notice about the oil? Are there bubbles in it?* If there are bubbles, watch them closely and see if they are rising or sinking. If they sink, they are actually water bubbles trapped inside the oil!

- Fill the eyedropper (or straw) with oil from the jar, and then slowly immerse it through the layer of oil, so that the dropper is visible in both the water layer at the bottom and the oil layer. Look at the dropper in the water layer, then in the oil layer. *What is different about the dropper in these two layers? Is it easier to see the dropper in the oil or the water?*

- With the bottom tip of the dropper in the water layer, squeeze the dropper to expel the oil inside and allow it to fill with water. Again, observe the oil dropper in the water and oil layers. *Is it easier to see the dropper in the oil or in the water this time?*

EXTRA

Try repeating this activity using glass objects, such as marbles, beads, glasses, or lenses. (Be sure you have permission to try out any object before using it.) Notice which things are the most difficult to see when you hold them in the oil versus the water. *Why do you think that is?*

OBSERVATIONS AND RESULTS

Did the eyedropper become invisible (or at least harder to see) when it was full of oil and immersed in oil? This is what is expected. It may also have been hard to see when it was in the water (and full of water) as well.

The eyedropper “disappears” because of how we see light as it encounters glass. When light hits a glass object, some of the light bounces (or reflects) off the glass. The rest of the light keeps going through the glass object, but the light is bent (or refracted) as it moves from the air to the glass.

The index of refraction for the oil is very close to the index of refraction for glass. Therefore, as light travels through the oil and into the glass eyedropper, very little of it is reflected or refracted. As a result, we see only the "ghost" of the eyedropper in the oil.

CLEANUP

Ask an adult to help you dispose of the oil and water mixture as oil may clog drains. Put away your other materials.

Colored Shadows

WHAT COLORS DO YOU SEE? USE COLORFUL SHADOWS TO EXPLORE HOW YOUR EYES DETECT A RAINBOW OF HUES. YOU CAN EVEN CREATE YOUR OWN BLENDS, PAINTING WITH LIGHT!

PROJECT TIME

20-25 minutes

KEY CONCEPTS

Light
Physics
Color
Eye

Have you ever wondered what the world would look like without colors? Most of us take them for granted because we see them everywhere: blue sky, green grass, yellow flowers, and countless more. Your eyes are actually able to distinguish up to 10 million colors! But where do all the colors come from? And how do our eyes detect them all? Find out with a little help from some shadows. Then you can paint with light—creating your own color blends by mixing red, green, and blue light!

BACKGROUND

Color vision has fascinated researchers for centuries. The scientific basis behind color is that visible light has wavelengths in the range of 400 to 700 nanometers. If light shines on an object, the object will absorb some light and reflect the rest of it. The wavelengths that are reflected are the ones that your eyes perceive and determine the color you will see. But how does the eye pick up the different wavelengths? For this, humans have special color receptor cells in the retinas of their eyes, called cone cells. There are three different kinds of cone cells. Each type responds to a specific spectrum wavelength and, therefore, is most sensitive to a certain color (red, green, or blue). Once light reaches your eye, each type of cone cell is stimulated differently by different wavelengths. The variance in signals from each cone allows the brain to perceive a continuous range of colors. But this requires blending colors to obtain different hues.

You have probably learned about the primary colors. Such colors can be combined and mixed to create a huge range of other colors. You can mix colors by additive or subtractive combination. Additive color combination happens when you overlap two or several beams of lights of different colors, a principle that is used in most electronic visual displays. Subtractive combination of colors happens when you shine a light through colored filters, which each will subtract (or absorb) some wavelengths of the original light. The commonly used primary colors for additive mixing are red, green (instead of yellow) and blue (which are the color ranges that your three different cone types are most sensitive to). By mixing them, you can create three secondary colors and one tertiary color. Get your flashlights ready and see for yourself!

MATERIALS

- A dark room
- One sheet of white paper or white poster board
- Three small flashlights with similar light intensities
- Blue, red, and green cellophane (available at most craft stores)
- Three rubber bands
- Pen
- Cardboard box
- Ruler or measuring tape
- Wide strip of paper about 2 inches (5 cm) wide (optional)

PREPARATION

- Cut five squares from each color of cellophane (red, blue and green) to a size that fits over the front end of your flashlight, with a little extra overlap.
- Take the five squares of one color and fold them over the front end of one of your flashlights. Put a rubber band around the colored cellophane pieces to keep them tightly attached to the flashlight.
- Do the same for the other two colors and flashlights.
- Set the sheet of white paper or poster board against a wall on a table, as a screen.
- Place the cardboard box in front of the white screen.
- Switch off all the lights in the room. (It should be relatively dark in order to see the color effects.)

PROCEDURE

- Take the "red" flashlight and switch it on. Point the light toward the white screen. *What color is the light that you see on the white paper?*
- With the light still turned on, rest the flashlight on the cardboard box. Adjust the distance between the box and the screen as well as the size of your light cone until you see a nice full circle of light on the white paper screen. Now, take your pen and hold it, vertically, between the flashlight and the white screen. *What do you see when you look at the screen? Is the shadow a specific color?*
- While keeping the pen in the same position, take the ruler and point one end of the ruler toward the center of the red flashlight. Point the other end toward the screen so it touches the shadow that you see on the screen. *Where is your pen located in relation to the ruler?*

- Switch the red flashlight off and repeat steps 1, 2, and 3 with the blue and the green flashlights, one at a time. *How does the light from each look on the screen? Does the color of the shadow change with the different colors? Is the pen always at the same location relative to the ruler?*

- Take the red and the green flashlights and switch them both on. Put the flashlights next to each other on the cardboard box so that they both point toward the screen. Make sure both light circles are the same size. Now move the red flashlight so that the red circle overlaps with the green one on the screen. *What happens to the green light once it overlaps with the red one? Does the color of the green light change? Which color does the circle on the screen have now?*

- With the green and red light still overlapping, take your pen again and hold it vertically in between the lights and the screen. *Do you see any shadows of the pen on the screen? How many are there? What colors are they?*

- Replace the green flashlight with the blue one. Place it on the cardboard box so that the blue and red circles overlap. *Does the combination of blue and red result in a different color? What does the color look like now?*

- Take your pen again and hold it, vertically, in between the lights and the screen. *How many shadows do you see this time? Did the colors of the shadows change again?*

- Now replace the red flashlight with the green one. Combine the color circles again on the white screen. *What color do you see now? Does it look very different from green and blue?*

- Finally, leave the green and the blue flashlight on the cardboard box and add the red one. Try to combine all three color circles into one. *What does the mixed color look like? Did you expect the color that you are seeing on the screen now? Why do you think the combination of all three colors results in this color?*

- Hold your pen vertically in between the three lights and the white screen. *What can you see on the screen? Is there more than one shadow? How many? And what are the colors of each of them? Where do you think they come from?*

SCIENCE FAIR PROJECT

With all three flashlights still switched on and combined into one circle of light on the screen, try to make shadows using a wider object than your pen, such as a wide strip of paper. When you hold the paper strip in between the light and the wall, vary the distance between your object and the screen. *Do the colors on the wall and the number of shadows change when you move your object closer to the screen? How many different colors can you create?*

EXTRA

Put all three flashlights on the cardboard box facing the screen. This time, point them in a way so that each of the colored circles overlap only partially with one another. *Which colors do you see where each circle overlaps with another? What do you see where all the circles overlap?*

SCIENCE FAIR PROJECT

Shine the green and the red flashlights on the white screen and combine their light beams. Take a ruler and put one end of the ruler at the center of the red light. Point the other end of the ruler toward the screen so it touches the white screen. Next, position your pen, vertically, right above the ruler, in between the lights and the screen and look at the shadows you see on the white screen. *What color is the shadow that the ruler touches on the screen? Can you explain why it has this color?* Now point the end of the ruler that was facing toward the red light toward the green light. *Where is the pen located now, in relation to the ruler?*

SCIENCE FAIR PROJECT

Instead of the white poster board, use different background colors. *Do you get different colored shadows?* Try also changing the colors of your flashlights. *Do different-colored lights alter your shadow color palette?*

OBSERVATIONS AND RESULTS

How many different-colored shadows did you create by mixing the colors? Probably many. This experiment is an example of additive color mixing, which means that you superimposed two or three beams of lights to mix them into a different color. Many television and computer monitors work that way to produce a variety of colors using only the primary colors red, blue, and green.

If you only had one light shining on your screen (red, blue, or green), the light on your screen should have had the same color. Holding the pen in between the light and the screen results in only one shadow, which is black. To understand shadows, you need to know that light travels in straight lines. You did see that when you connected the light source with the shadow on the wall using a ruler. You might have noticed that the pen is always directly on the same line as the ruler, which means that the shadow on the wall is created exactly where the pen blocks out all the light from the flashlight. Now, when you started to combine two colors, the spots on the wall should have changed into a different color. Each combination of lights results in a different stimulation of your cone cells, and depending on the signals that those cells send to your brain, you perceive a different color. Red and green combine into yellow; red and blue become a pinkish color, called magenta; and blue and green turn into a light blue-green, called cyan. These colors are all called secondary colors because they are each the product of two primary colors. A nice way to show all primary, secondary, and tertiary colors from red, blue, and green is to only partially overlap all the three light circles on the screen.

When you put the pen in between two combined colors of light and the wall, you saw two shadows; each one has the color of one of the two light sources. Again, this is due to the fact that light travels in straight lines, and if you did the extra activity, you should have seen that if you put your pen directly on the line of the ruler pointing from the red flashlight to the wall, the shadow created at the other end of the ruler should have been green. This means that on the path along the ruler, the pen blocked out the red light and created a shadow. When you pointed the ruler to the green flashlight, however, you might have noticed that the pathway of the green light was not blocked by the pen, which is why the shadow looked green. When you added the third color, combining all three primary colors, the resulting color was white. We perceive the color "white" when all types of cone cells are stimulated equally, which is the case when you combine all three primary colors.

CLEANUP

Turn off the flashlights and recycle any colored paper you used during the experiment.

THE SCIENTIFIC METHOD

The scientific method helps scientists—and students—gather facts to prove whether an idea is true. Using this method, scientists come up with ideas and then test those ideas by observing facts and drawing conclusions. You can use the scientific method to develop and test your own ideas!

Question: What do you want to learn? What problem needs to be solved? Be as specific as possible.
Research: Learn more about your topic and refine your question.
Hypothesis: Form an educated guess about what you think will answer your question. This allows you to make a prediction you can test.
Experiment: Create a test to learn if your hypothesis is correct. Limit the number of variables, or elements of the experiment that could change.
Analysis: Record your observations about the progress and results of your experiment. Then analyze your data to understand what it means.
Conclusion: Review all your data. Did the results of the experiment match the prediction? If so, your hypothesis was correct. If not, your hypothesis may need to be changed.

GLOSSARY

absorb: To take in.
assumption: Something that is believed to be true, but could not be true.
atmosphere: The mixture of gases that surround a planet.
disperse: To go in different directions.
distort: To make the regular appearance of something strange or different.
fluorescent: Brightly colored.
molecule: A very small piece of matter.
nerve: A part of the body that sends messages to the brain and allows something to feel things.
opaque: Unable to be seen through.
optics: The study of light, its behaviors, and its properties.
parallel: Lying in the same direction as another thing.
pedestrian: A person who is walking.
perpendicular: Being at right angles.
phenomenon: A fact or an event that is observed.
physics: The study of matter, energy, force, and motion, and the relationship among them.
principle: A basic theory.
transparent: Letting light shine through.
reflect: To throw back light.
retina: A part of your eye that helps take in images to send to the brain.

ADDITIONAL RESOURCES

Books

Colin, Stuart. *The Speed of Starlight.* Somerville, MA: Big Picture Press, 2019.

Ferrie, Chris. *Let's Make a Rainbow!: Seeing the Science of Light Refraction with Optical Physics.* Naperville, IL: Sourcebooks Explore, 2020.

Gardner, Jane P. *Light and Sound.* Minneapolis, MN: Bearport Publishing Company, 2023.

Websites

Discovery Education
sciencefaircentral.com

Exploratorium
https://www.exploratorium.edu/search/science%20fair%20projects

Science Buddies
https://www.sciencebuddies.org/science-fair-projects/project-ideas/list

Science Fun
https://www.sciencefun.org/?s=science+fair

Videos

How Rainbows Form | Physics Girl
ny.pbslearningmedia.org/resource/rainbows-formation-physicsgirl-video-1010/how-rainbows-form-physics-girl/

Light and Color
https://ny.pbslearningmedia.org/resource/lsps07.sci.phys.energy.lightcolor/light-and-color/

Light: Let There Be Light | Science Trek
https://ny.pbslearningmedia.org/resource/light-color-science-trek/light-color-science-trek/

INDEX